NUTS

BY OLIVE L. EARLE
with Michael Kantor

illustrated by Olive L. Earle

William Morrow and Company
New York   1975

Printed in the United States of America.

1 2 3 4 5   79 78 77 76 75

Library of Congress Cataloging in Publication Data

Earle, Olive Lydia.
   Nuts.

   SUMMARY: Briefly discusses the characteristics
of thirty-three different kinds of nuts, the plants on which
they grow, and their various uses.
   1. Nuts—Juvenile literature. [1. Nuts] I. Kantor,
Michael (date), joint author. II. Title.
QK660.E27   582'.16   74-26800
ISBN 0-688-22025-8
ISBN 0-688-32025-2 lib. bdg.

ALSO BY OLIVE L. EARLE

Birds and Their Beaks
Birds and Their Nests
Birds of the Crow Family
Camels and Llamas
Crickets
The Octopus
Paws, Hoofs, and Flippers
Peas, Beans, and Licorice
Pond and Marsh Plants
Praying Mantis
Robins in the Garden
The Rose Family
Scavengers
Squirrels in the Garden
State Birds and Flowers
State Trees
Strange Companions in Nature
Strange Fishes of the Sea
Strange Lizards

WITH MICHAEL KANTOR

Animals and Their Ears

Seeds of plants have almost numberless shapes and sizes. In every seed there is the beginning stage of a new plant. This embryo is surrounded by the special food needed for its development, and it is protected by various types of outer covering. People usually refer to any seed with a hard overcoat as a nut. But botanists, the people who study plants, have a special way of defining a nut, and all seeds that are covered by a hard shell are not true nuts. To a scientist, a true nut is a hard-shelled, one-seeded fruit that does not split open when it is ripe; it keeps its seed within itself until the embryo sprouts and pushes its way out of its covering. Acorns and hickories, for instance, are true nuts. A peanut is not.

This book describes so-called nuts as well as true nuts. In most cases both kinds are good to eat and provide valuable food.

acorn

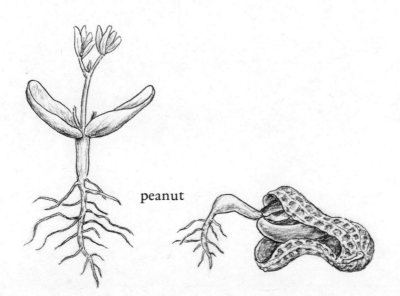

peanut

Botanists have special names for the various parts of plants and for the different ways in which they grow.

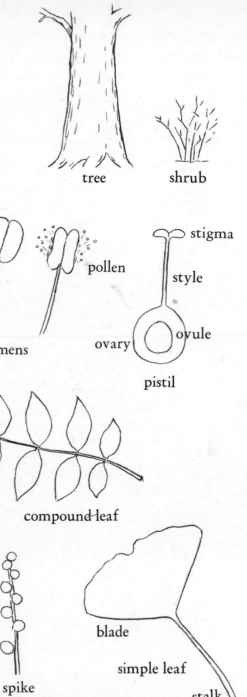

tree

shrub

petal

anther

filament

stamens

pollen

stigma

style

ovule

ovary

pistil

sepal

flower

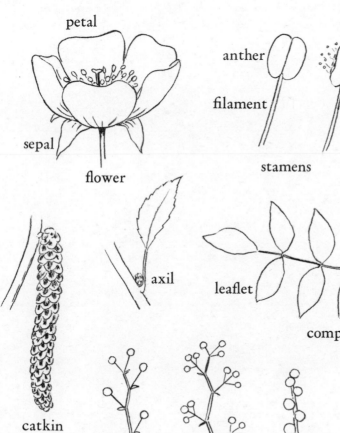

catkin

axil

leaflet

compound leaf

raceme

panicle

spike

blade

simple leaf

stalk

In the United States there are at least fifty different kinds of oak trees. Most of them have leaves with scalloped edges, and, without exception, oaks of every species bear acorns. Though an acorn does not look like a typical nut, botanists classify it as a nut because of the way it is constructed; over the interior kernel, it has a hard shell that does not split open.

Without the usual scallops at the margins of their leaves, the willow oak and the live oak, at home in mild climates,

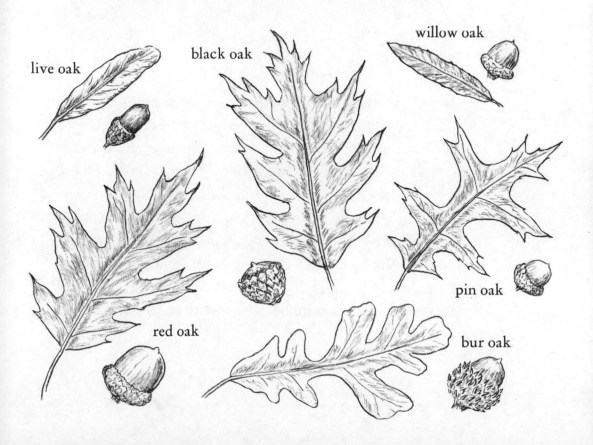

live oak

black oak

willow oak

red oak

pin oak

bur oak

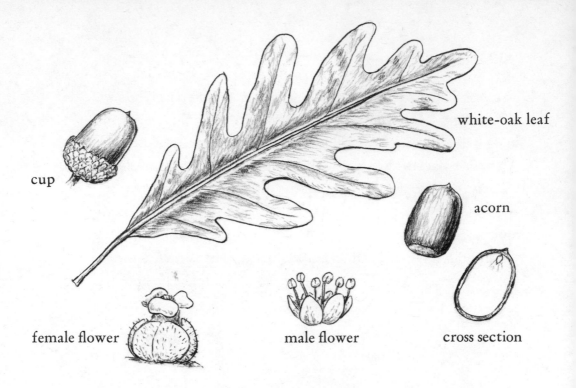

cup

white-oak leaf

acorn

female flower

male flower

cross section

are called *evergreen.* Throughout the year, new leaves replace the old ones and their branches are never bare. Most of the other oaks shed their leaves in the autumn; some, such as the white oak, retain their withered leaves until the spring, when swelling buds push them off.

In the spring, the flowers of oaks appear. The tiny male pollen-bearing ones are borne in strings that are called *catkins.* Nearby a small cluster of female flowers appears. Each fertilized one will ultimately develop into an acorn that is set in a cup formed by a rosette of tiny leaflets, or bracts. Some acorn cups are shallow, some deep. On some, the overlapping bracts are hairy, and certain cups wear a fringe of bristles. Others are without any such trimmings. The acorns of some oaks ripen by the end of summer, while others take two seasons to mature. Some are bitter; others are not.

At one time, native American tribes used acorns as a staple food. They are enjoyed by squirrels and other animals. Birds, too, carry off acorns. Often a squirrel or a jay may be responsible for the appearance of a stray oak seedling in a garden that is far from the parent tree A squirrel may forget to dig up an acorn that it has buried in a flower bed. A jay flying to a convenient perch may drop its meal, and the nut falls to a spot suitable for its sprouting. In such a place, the acorn sends out from its pointed end a stem that grows upward and a root that grows downward.

Usually an oak tree is about ten years of age before it bears acorns. It continues to produce fruit for a great many years, for the trees are long-lived; some are known to have flourished for centuries.

ALMOND

Almond trees, widely cultivated in mild climates, are closely related to peach trees. The pink flowers, each with five petals, are similar, but the fruits are very different. The peach's juicy, good-to-eat pulp is, in the almond, replaced by a thick, hard husk. At maturity, this case splits to release the nut that contains the edible seed—the nutmeat.

There are various kinds of almonds. Some nuts have hard shells, and others are known as *soft-shelled* or *paper-shelled*. The meat of some almonds is sweet. In others it is bitter. The kernels of bitter almonds contain prussic acid; this poison is removed if oil from the nutmeats is to be used in flavoring extracts. Sweet almonds are used in all sorts of confectionery. The thin, brown skin on the meat slips off easily after the kernel is put in scalding water for a few moments.

A typical almond tree grows from twenty to thirty feet in height and, in general appearance, is similar to the peach tree. An almond tree only produces nuts in areas where a late frost will not destroy the flowers.

BEECH NUT

The American beech-tree, with its smooth, silvery bark, grows wild in the United States from the east as far west as Texas. It may reach a height of sixty or more feet. The leaves, three to six inches long, have sharply toothed edges and noticeable parallel veins. Withered leaves often hang on the tree far into the winter.

In the spring, when the leaves are only partly unfolded, the flowers appear. The male flowers form a fluffy ball at the tip of a hanging stem. The female flowers, usually in pairs, grow near the end of young twigs.

After a brief flowering, the ovary of a fertilized flower forms a bur covered with slender prickles; inside it are two small nuts. When it is ripe, the bur splits into four sections to release the three-sided nuts; each is less than an inch in length. The shell of each of these seeds is somewhat leathery, and inside the shell is the kernel, which is good to eat. The fallen nuts are known as *beech mast* and were once used extensively as food for pigs. Animals, wild turkeys, and other birds feast on beach mast.

The copper beech bears similar nuts. The tree is of European origin, but it is now planted here for the sake of the beautiful color of its reddish, copper-colored leaves.

BETEL NUT

The betel nut is the seed of an areca palm that abounds in tropical Asia. Up to one hundred feet in height, the tree has a slender, straight trunk topped with huge leaves. Each compound leaf may be six feet in length and is made up of many leaflets. Sprouting below the leafstalks, the sprays of white flowers are protected by a sheath known as a *spathe*. The fertilized female flowers produce the fruit. About the size of a hen's egg, a mature fruit is orange red and has a soft, fibrous husk about one-half-inch thick covering the seed—the betel nut.

Many Oriental peoples chew the betel nut as a stimulant. To prepare a package of it for such use, scrapings of the nut are wrapped in the leaves of a plant called *betel pepper*. These leaves are moistened with lime. This Oriental form of chewing gum has been popular for many hundreds of years despite the fact that its constant use blackens, and finally destroys, the teeth of those who chew it.

fruit

ripe fruit cut open

The shrub commonly named the American bladdernut grows up to fifteen feet in height. Its leaves are made up of three broad, pointed leaflets. Each small flower, about one-half inch long, has five sepals, five white petals, and five pollen-bearing stamens. Its three pistils are joined at the base to form the seed-bearing ovary. The flowers are borne in a raceme pattern at the end of a nodding stem. Sometimes the flower buds are pickled and used as a substitute for the buds of the caper bush, a native of Mediterranean areas. Capers are used in salad dressing and in cookery.

The plant's name comes from its unusual fruit that, when mature, is a much-inflated papery pod up to two inches long. Inside this capsule, there are a few nutlike, hard-coated seeds. Though the nuts are edible, they are not used as food, because they tend to act as a laxative.

The American bladdernut stands cold weather well and is planted in gardens as an ornamental shrub.

BRAZIL NUT
Cream nut

The tree whose seed is the Brazil nut will not thrive in a cold climate. As its name indicates, it is a native of Brazil, where forests of the giant trees grow on the banks of the Amazon and the Rio Grande. A tree may reach a height of one hundred and fifty feet, and it has huge leaves that may be two feet long, though only about six inches broad. The cream-colored flowers, blooming on an upright stem, have six petals. A fertilized flower produces a round seed vessel about six inches in diameter and weighing more than two pounds. The two-layered, woody, outer covering of the seeds is stone hard, and a heavy hammer or sharp axe is needed to open it. Inside this protective case, there are eighteen to twenty-four closely packed seeds. These seeds are the Brazil nuts sold in stores. Each has a hard, wrinkled shell and is three sided; inside the shell is the pure-white kernel that is delicious to eat and has a high fat content. The meat yields a great deal of oil, which is good for burning and is used in salad oil, lubricants, and paints.

Growing in remote areas of Brazil is a tree bearing nuts with kernels similar to those of the common Brazil nut. It is named the monkey-pot tree because the seed vessel looks as though it were made of rusty iron, and it is so large that if he thought of it, a monkey could use it as a pot. It has a lid that drops off when the nuts are ripe.

BUCKEYE
OHIO BUCKEYE, SWEET BUCKEYE

The various species of buckeye trees belong to the horse chestnut family. Perhaps the most famous of the group is the Ohio buckeye, which Ohio chose as its state tree. Early settlers are said to have found the plentiful tree useful in all sorts of ways.

The Ohio buckeye differs from the horse chestnut in not having sticky winter buds. And there are usually only five leaflets making up a leaf. The greenish yellow flowers grow in a long cluster called a *panicle.* Male and female flowers grow on the same panicle. The husks, containing the seeds, have sparse prickles. Inside the bur, there is usually one nut. Occasionally there are two. Though the kernels are bitter, they are eaten by animals.

The sweet buckeye is the largest of the species; it reaches a possible height of ninety feet. Though the nuts are supposedly sweet, they are not sweet enough for most people's taste. They have to be boiled or roasted before being eaten. Animals, however, will feast on raw nuts.

sweet buckeye

In many ways the sweet buckeye is similar to the Ohio tree, but its larger, roundish fruit has a thicker husk that is without prickles. Usually it contains two nuts, each about one and one-half inches long. Cattle and pigs find them good food.

Ohio buckeye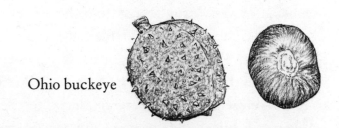

CANDLENUT
Kukui

The candlenut tree was of great value to early Hawaiians, who benefited from it in many ways. In commemoration, it has been chosen as the state tree of the Hawaiian Islands. The name of candlenut comes from the use of its fruit as a source of light; the kernel of the nut contains an oil that burns readily. Various methods of using the nut as a candle were devised, from burning the whole dried nut to lighting an oil-soaked wick set in a stone holder.

The tree bears clusters of male and female creamy white flowers. The male flowers have about eleven stamens that supply pollen; the female flowers have an ovary that, only after fertilization, will become a mature fruit nearly two inches in diameter. The somewhat walnutlike seed is inside a thin nutshell, which, in turn, is protected by a hard, green outer husk. The kernels are edible when roasted, but when eaten raw they act as a purging medicine. A permanent oil, used by artists, is pressed from the nuts, and dye is obtained from them also.

The candlenut tree averages about fifty feet in height. It is never without leaves so is considered an evergreen. Originally a native of Old World tropics and subtropics, the tree is now widely distributed in frost-free regions.

The various species of tung trees are closely related to

the candlenut, which is sometimes listed as a tung tree. All of them are famous for the oil that their seeds contain. A Chinese tung tree, shaped like an apple tree, is cultivated in warm sections of the United States. The mature fruit of this tree is about the size of a large plum; the hard, shell-like husk contains three to seven seeds. These tung nuts are pressed to draw out the valuable oil. Tung oil is used in varnishes, paints, and for waterproofing. The leftover meat is used as a fertilizer.

CASHEW NUT

The cashew nut seems to grow in a very curious way, for it looks as though it were attached to the end of a pulpy fruit. Though referred to as the cashew apple, the growth is not a fruit, but is the swollen end of a flower stalk. The fragrant, pinkish flowers grow in a panicle at the end of a young branch. A flower fades, its stem swells, and, in time, its seed becomes a cashew nut. The red or yellow cashew apple may reach the size of a small pear; rather acid in flavor, it is sometimes used for making jelly. Embedded in its thick end is the base of the nut that is about the size of a large bean. The nut has a double shell; between its outer and inner layer there is a disagreeable juice that is avoided for it may cause damage to human skin. The kernel of the nut is rich in oil and, after being roasted, is very good to eat.

The forty-foot-tall cashew tree is never bare of leaves and so is considered an evergreen. The leathery leaves, up to

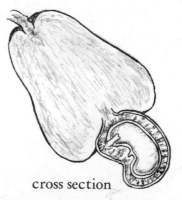

cross section

eight inches long, are oval in shape. Though the cashew is a native of tropical America, it has become naturalized in many frost-free lands. Prized for its valuable nuts, the tree also yields a gum from its bark, which is used in medicine.

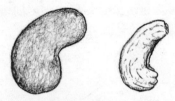

CHESTNUT, AMERICAN

The story of the American chestnut tree is a sad one. In earlier times the hundred-foot-tall tree was common throughout eastern and mideastern United States. Animals and people enjoyed its fruits. At the beginning of this century, the trees were attacked by a blight caused by a fungus. The disease spread rapidly and, over the years, practically all were destroyed. Some of the old roots continue to send up shoots bearing six-inch-long narrow leaves, and occasionally a few nuts form. But these adventurous sprouts are attacked by blight and do not survive for long. A Japanese variety of chestnut, more resistant to blight, is now being grown here to a limited extent.

The chestnuts sold in markets are imported from Europe. These nuts, with shells and skins removed, frequently are used in poultry stuffing, or they are cooked and mashed for use in all sorts of desserts. Their food value is high, for they are rich in carbohydrates and proteins.

Chestnuts develop from female flowers that grow near the top of a string of male ones; the catkin is from six to eight inches long. A few of the female flowers' ovaries

develop into spine-covered burs; inside each there are two or three seeds. When ripe, the seeds become the familiar brown nuts. Often one side of a nut is flattened due to pressure while it was growing in the bur. With the coming of frost, the bur splits and the nuts fall out.

CHINQUAPIN, COMMON

The chinquapins are closely related to the chestnut, but most of them grow as shrubs rather than trees. One species, the common chinquapin, does grow as a spreading tree and may reach a height of forty feet. Its leaves are shaped like chestnut leaves, but they are smaller. The pattern of male and female flowers is like that of the chestnut, but the burs, covered with stiff spines, are smaller than chestnut burs. Each bur contains a single nut, which is bright brown and shiny; at its tip, there is often seen the dried pistil that received the pollen while the chinquapin was in flower. The edible kernel is very sweet. The common, or tree, chinquapin is found mainly in Southeastern and Gulf states.

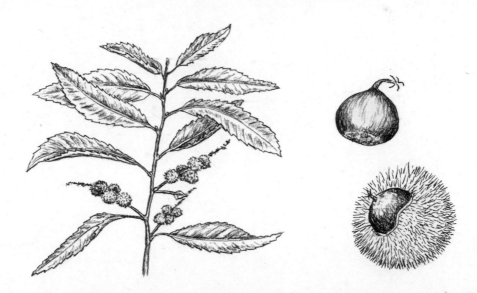

COCONUT

Coconuts are the fruit of a palm tree that is at home in frost-free parts of the world. The coconut palm is considered one of man's most valuable trees, for all of it is useful. Bits of root are used as a sort of chewing gum. The trunk provides wood. The leaves are used for thatching houses, for making mats, and for weaving baskets. The nut is famous as a source of food; it contains energy-giving fat and carbohydrates. When the meat is dried, it is known as *copra.* The oil extracted from copra is used in soap, face creams, butter substitutes, and many other products. The residue is fed

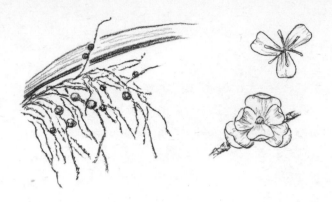

to cattle in the form of oil cakes. The coarse fibers of the husk, called *coir,* are spun into rope and are used for making mats and brushes. The hard coconut shell often is fashioned into bowls and ladles.

A leaf of the coconut palm may be twelve to twenty feet long and is made up of many leaflets that are two to three feet in length. Sprouting some sixty feet from ground level, the leaves form a crown at the top of a branchless trunk. The flower sprays grow from the bases of the lower leaves; the branched spray is called a *panicle.* The male, pollen-bearing flowers are nearer the tip of each branchlet than are the female flowers whose ovaries, when fertilized, produce the seed-bearing fruit. Each one grows and grows until it becomes almost the size of a man's head. A coconut palm may continuously produce nuts that are in various stages of development, and, in the course of a year, a tree may yield from eighty to one hundred nuts.

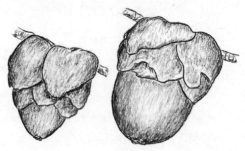

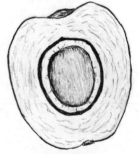

cross section

As a ripening coconut develops, it contains a nutritious liquid known as *coconut milk.* Surrounding the milk is a half-inch-thick layer of meat, which is the part of the nut used in all sorts of confectionery. The meat in its natural state acts as food for the beginning stage of a tree. It is guarded by a hard, woody shell, which, in turn, is embedded in a green, fibrous husk. This thick husk is sufficiently waterproof to protect the nut should it fall in water and enables it to float a short distance before it rots away. Perhaps it will be washed up on a nearby sandy shore, where it will sprout. If it thrives, it will produce nuts when it is ten years old. The new young palm tree sprouts from the largest of the three eyes that can be seen at the base of the coconut.

COCONUT, SEYCHELLES

Double coconut

The Seychelles coconut is notable in many ways. The palm tree that bears it grows in one locality only, the Seychelles Islands in the Indian Ocean. This peculiar isolation has come about because the seed-bearing fruit, falling into the sea, disintegrates before it reaches a distant shore. Borne on a female tree, this fruit is thought to be the largest in the world; it may weigh forty to fifty pounds and be as much as eighteen inches in width. The fruit is constricted down its center and looks somewhat like two coconuts glued together. Thus, it has earned the name of double coconut, even though it is not a true coconut.

Ten years are needed for the fruit to mature from flower to ripe nut. A smooth, green husk covers the hard-shelled nut, which contains a sweet, white jelly. Later the jelly changes to a horny kernel that is too hard to be used for food. The tree that produces this strange nut takes thirty years to bear blossoms and a century to reach its full height of about one hundred feet. It belongs to the fan palm group,

and its branchless, comparatively slender trunk is topped
with a crown of enormous leaves whose stems may be fifteen
feet long. The leaflets that make up the fan grow to a
possible twenty feet in length.

young tree

COLA NUT
Kola nut

The cola nut is the seed of a tree that originally was a native of western tropical Africa. Varieties now are cultivated in many regions where the climate is sufficiently warm. A favored species is shaped like an apple tree and grows to a height of forty feet. Its leathery leaves are up to six inches long. The yellow flowers are borne in clusters of twelve or more. A cola flower has no petals, their place being taken by the expanded tips of their five sepals. After fertilization, the ovary matures and becomes a hollow, fibrous capsule with, usually, five brown seeds inside it; each is about the size of a horse chestnut. Although in their natural state cola nuts are bitter, native people chew them as a stimulant. When the kernels are treated in a special manner, they yield an extract containing caffeine, which is used in soft drinks and in some medicines.

The cola-nut tree is related to the cacao tree whose roasted seeds are the source of cocoa and chocolate.

GINKGO NUT

Maidenhair tree

The edible seeds of the ginkgo tree are often referred to as nuts. These so-called nuts are borne on female trees. The male tree's pollen-bearing stamens grow in a catkinlike arrangement. The beginning of a nut sprouts from a knob, called a *spur,* that protrudes from a branch. By the end of summer, the fruitstalk has lengthened and has one or occasionally two fully developed fruits at its tip.

Contained in a yellowish, soft pulp, the ginkgo's seed is up to an inch in length; it is oblong in shape and has a thin, silver-white shell. Inside the shell is the sweet, starchy kernel. After roasting, the nuts are enjoyed by Chinese and Japanese people, who have cultivated the trees for centuries. Ginkgos are not found growing wild.

The foul odor of fallen fruits that have broken open makes the planting of female trees undesirable in the United States,

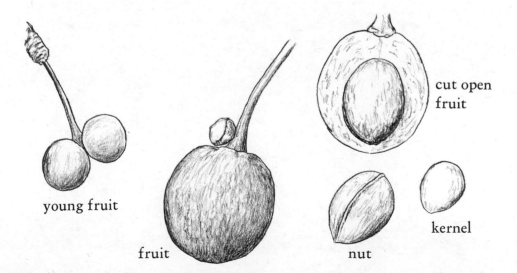

young fruit

fruit

cut open fruit

nut

kernel

but male trees are frequently grown in Eastern states as ornamentals. They are in high favor because they withstand smog, disease, and attack by insect pests. The name of maidenhair tree comes from the leaves being shaped like the much smaller leaflets of the maidenhair fern.

The ginkgo may reach a height of about eighty feet; as the tree ages, its straight branches spread out irregularly, changing its shape from its earlier pyramid design. The tree is easy to recognize because of its unusul, fan-shaped leaves, which are from two to four inches across. A leaf may be notched at its upper edge, and its stalk may be longer than its blade.

The ginkgo tree, brought to this country from the Orient, has an unusual history; fossilized leaves, found in rocks, show that the tree flourished millions of years ago, and the leaf's shape has not changed since prehistoric days.

maidenhair fern

HAZELNUT

The American hazelnut grows wild in many eastern parts
of the United States, where a second species, the beaked
hazelnut, is less common. These two are the only hazelnuts
that are natives of this country. Sometimes the name of
hazelnut is given to closely related foreign species, such as
the filbert, the cobnut, and the Barcelona nut. They all belong to the *Corylus* genus, and this botanical name is from
a Greek word meaning *helmet.* It describes the leaflike husk
that covers the mature, hard-shelled nut.

The American hazelnut is a shrub or small, bushy tree
that thrives in clumps and thickets at the edge of woods. The
plant may reach a height of six feet, and its heart-shaped
leaves, which have saw-toothed edges, are up to five inches
long. Before the leaves appear, the hazel's flowers are in
bloom. Formed the previous years, the long, hanging catkins
of male flowers are ready to shed their pollen in March or
early April. The female flowers are like tiny buds with red
stigmas protruding from them. As a fertilized flower de-

beaked hazelnut

velops, two of the inner scales that surround the ovary en-
large to become a stiffish, split-edged covering; this "helmet"
often completely encloses the mature nut.

Roundish oval in shape, a ripe nut is about one-half inch
high and has a rough base marking the place where it was
attached to the husk. The meat inside the woody shell is
very good to eat. One half of its weight is made up of oil;
this oil is used in perfumes, in medicines, and is valued as
an artist's oil. Hazel stems are in demand for the making of
artists' charcoal sticks.

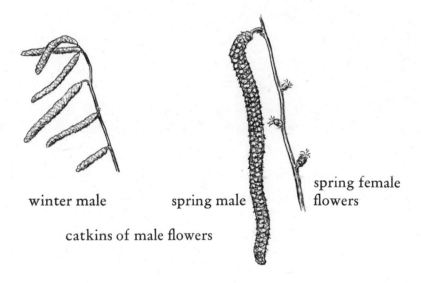

winter male   spring male   spring female
                                              flowers

catkins of male flowers

HICKORY NUT

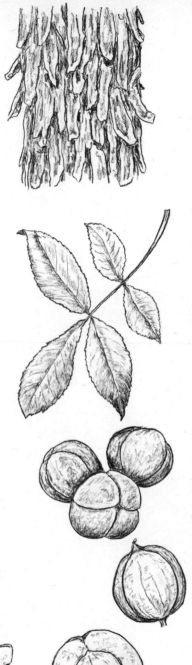

There are a number of different kinds of hickory trees that are natives of the eastern United States. Local names are used for many of them. Botanists call one important hickory, *Carya ovata;* its popular name of shagbark describes the tree's trunk. Light gray on a mature tree, the bark is broken into thick, flat flakes; these flakes curl outward, particularly at their lower ends, and give a shaggy look to the trunk.

The nuts of *Carya ovata* are produced in typical hickory fashion. They develop from fertilized female flowers, which grow in spikes near the catkins formed of strings of male flowers. The fruit's thick husk splits into four sections to release the shell that protects the seed—the nutmeat. There may be considerable variation in the shape of the nuts, but all contain delicious kernels that have, in concentrated form, fat, protein, and carbohydrates.

Besides bearing edible nuts, this hickory's timber is commercially important. Strong and springy, it is used for golf clubs, axe handles,

and other implements. The smoke from burning hickory logs gives cured meat a special flavor.

Among the various species in the *Carya* group there are some, such as the pecan, pignut, and bitternut, that have thin husks. The shagbark and the mockernut have thick husks.

HORSE CHESTNUT

The horse chestnut is not related to the American chestnut. No one is sure how the tree got its name; perhaps it comes from the scar, left on a branch after a leaf has fallen, which is shaped rather like a horseshoe and shows marks that imitate nail holes. The tree is not a native one and is thought to have originated in Asia. In many countries, the common horse chestnut and a red variety are planted in parks and along streets. A tree sometimes reaches a height of one hundred feet.

A horse chestnut leaf is usually made up of seven leaflets, though sometimes there are only five. When the tree is in full leaf, numberless erect pyramids of flowers come into bloom. Each flower on the possibly twelve-inch-tall cluster has either four or five white petals blotched with yellow and red; the petals are unequal in size and shape. The noticeable, protruding stamens have red pollen. The flowers

at the top of the pyramid are male flowers, while those on the lower part have both stamens and ovaries; when fertilized, an ovary will produce the tree's seed, which is a chestnut.

During the summer, the fruit, with thick spines, develops quickly and becomes a full-grown green bur. Inside its three joined outer walls, called *valves,* there are one or more shiny, brown nuts. Many animals enjoy the nuts, but people find them too bitter to eat.

In winter, the horse chestnut tree is easy to recognize, for big, brown, sticky buds, growing opposite each other on a smooth twig, are identifying signs. These are leaf buds. The extra large bud at the tip of the twig is the one that contains the beginnings of the pyramid of flowers.

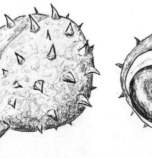

The palm tree that bears ivory nuts has a botanical name meaning *elephant plant*. The reference is to the nut's hard, white kernel, which, because it mimics the ivory of an elephant's tusk, is known as *vegetable ivory*. Man uses it to make buttons and various other imitation ivory articles.

The flowers, which precede the fruits, are crowded together on a spike, and, at maturity, the fruits are in a closely packed group. Each knobby husk generally contains a number of oval nuts about the size of a hen's egg. Inside a nut's shell is the valuable kernel.

Instead of growing upright, this palm's short trunk lies along the ground. At its tip there is a big tuft of huge leaves, each made up of a great many light green leaflets; the top of the crown may be thirty or forty feet from the ground. The tree is a native of warm parts of South America.

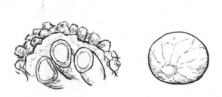

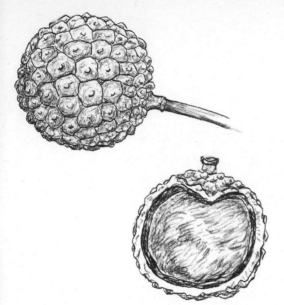

LITCHI NUT
Lichee, Leechee

For the sake of its delicious fruit, the litchi tree has been cultivated in the Orient for at least fifteen hundred years. It is now grown in other regions where the humidity is high and the summers long and hot. The fruit, thought of as a nut, is an inch or more in diameter and has a thin shell, rough and brittle. Inside this crust, and covering a smooth, hard-shelled seed, is a juicy, white pulp, which is edible and contains a great deal of sugar. The pulp may be eaten fresh, or the nuts may be dried; after drying, the pulp becomes firm and turns to a dark brown color. Dried litchis are exported to be sold in stores that specialize in Oriental foods. Occasionally the shelled fruit is available, packed with syrup in glass jars.

The litchi tree is a large evergreen with long, oval leaves. The panicles of white flowers grow in the angle formed by the leafstalk and a branch, the axil, or the flower sprays sprout at the tip of a branch. After the fruits form and are ripening, a cluster may be enclosed in a woven bamboo basket for protection against flying foxes, which are fruit-eating bats.

MACADAMIA NUT

Queensland nut

Native to Australia, the macadamia tree's seed is a nut
with a pleasantly flavored, nutritious kernel; its fat content
is over seventy percent. Of the several known species, two
are commercially grown in orchards. One of them has a
rough, leathery, often-pointed husk, and the tree's glossy,
dark green leaves have prickly edges. The other has round,
smooth fruit, and the leaves have no prickles.

Macadamia leaves are from eight to twelve inches long.
The flowers, either creamy or pinkish, are borne in hanging
catkins that are often as long as the leaves; each flower has
both an ovary and stamens. A fertilized flower develops into
a fruit whose husk splits into two valves to release the mature
nut. At harvest time, the fallen nuts are picked up by hand.
The hard-shelled nuts, about one inch in diameter, are dried
before being cracked open. The white kernels are then
roasted and salted and are ready for people to enjoy.

Macadamias are now cultivated in Hawaii, and the tree is sometimes planted in Southern California as an ornamental evergreen. Long ago macadamia trees were discovered in a coastal rain forest, and they thrive best where there is plenty of moisture in the soil. The often round-topped tree may reach forty or more feet in height, and sometimes it has more than one trunk. The tree is named after an Australian scientist, John Macadam, who lived more than a century ago.

kernel

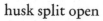

husk split open

Even the most adventurous monkey would hesitate before trying to climb a monkey-puzzle tree, for each of its branches is surrounded by closely set, prickle-tipped leaves arranged in a spiral pattern. The two-inch-long leaf is flat and stiff, with its pointed end overlapping the leaf above it. The leaves are long-lived and may remain on a branch for ten or more years. The seeds of the tree are held in a roundish-oval cone, about seven inches long, which falls apart at maturity. Each of the cone's scales, tipped with a sharp spine, covers a wedge-shaped, inch-long seed, which is referred to as a nut. As many as three hundred of them may be in one cone, and there may be thirty huge cones on a tree. The nuts have a pleasant flavor and are eaten raw, boiled, or roasted; they are an important food for local people.

The monkey-puzzle tree is a native of the Chilean Andes, where it may

reach a height of well over one hundred feet in the forest. Its trunk is straight, and at its top there is a crown of branches. A young tree, flourishing in an open area, is shaped rather like a round-topped pyramid with some of its branches almost at ground level.

The monkey-puzzle tree thrives in gardens where the winters are sufficiently mild. It is related to the Norfolk Island pine, which is often grown as a house plant.

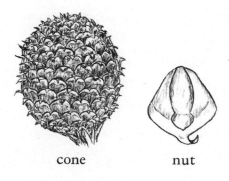

cone   nut

NUT GRASS, CHUFA

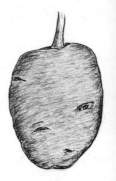

potato

The various nut grasses are members of the sedge family; in this huge group, there are some three thousand species found throughout the world. In warm regions some of the nut grasses are grown for the sake of the edible tubers they bear. (A tuber is a thickened portion of an underground stem; it is a storehouse of food, and from it new plants grow. The potato is an example of a tuber.)

One nut grass, named chufa, grows wild in certain parts of the United States. Its oblong so-called nuts are about three quarters of an inch in length. Because the tubers are a favorite food of hogs, the grass is planted in some places. Occasionally people eat them either raw or baked, and they have used them as a substitute for coffee. The tubers have a fine flavor and contain considerable amounts of oil, starch, and sugar. Cultivated plants may create a problem because of their habit of spreading over land needed for other crops, and, once established, the chufa is difficult to eradicate. With long grasslike leaves, the plant grows from one to three feet tall and has spikes of small flowers at the top of a central stalk.

Chufa has a famous relative, the papyrus. The pith of this eight-foot-tall sedge was used by early Egyptians to make a type of writing paper.

NUTMEG

Nutmeg is the kernel of the fruit of various related species of tropical trees. Among the species, one is valued above the others as the source of the grated nutmeg used as a flavoring spice. The fruit of this tree, golden yellow when ripe, is about the size of a walnut. Under its husk there is a layer of pulp, and, set in the pulp, there is a stringy red case, which envelops the shell containing the seed. This well-protected seed is the nutmeg. The red sheath is valued also; it is dried and ground into powder to be used as a spice with the name of mace.

The commercially grown nutmeg tree reaches a height of about twenty-five feet. Clusters of tiny white flowers sprout at the place where a leafstalk joins a stem. Male flowers grow on one tree, female flowers on another. A male flower provides pollen to fertilize a female flower, whose ovary is the origin of the fruit.

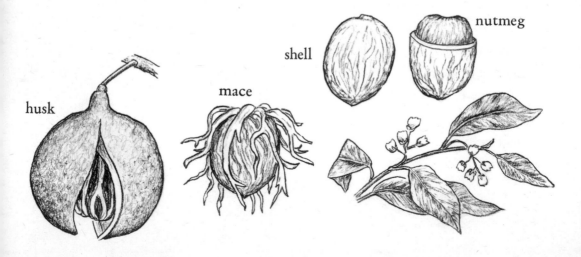

husk

mace

shell

nutmeg

PEANUT
Goober

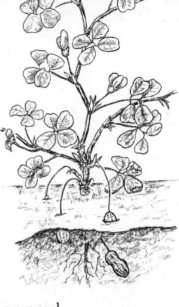

The peanut does not grow on a tree; it grows underground. It is the seed of a two-foot-high, spreading plant that is related to peas and beans. Unlike these legumes whose fruit is visible, the peanut has the habit of pushing its seed pods into the earth, where they develop out of sight. The pods originate in bright yellow flowers, which spring from the angle formed by leafstalk and stem. After the flower has been fertilized and its petals have fallen, its stalk lengthens, and the expanding pod tunnels its way into the soil. The mature pod, often constricted in the middle, has a brittle, wrinkled shell with one to three so-called nuts inside it. Rich in protein and fat, they are roasted for human food, and the ground-up seeds often are eaten in the form of peanut butter. Oil is extracted from peanuts to be used in all manner of ways, from salad oil to soap. The whole plant sometimes is used as animal fodder.

The peanut is thought to have originated in Brazil, but it is now grown in all warm regions of the world.

PEANUT, HOG

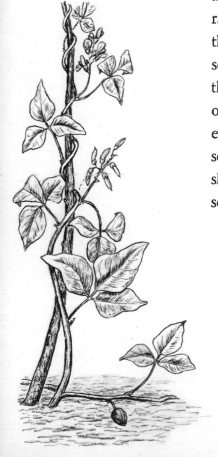

The well-known peanut has a less famous, less nutritious relative named the *hog peanut*. It is supposed to be relished by hogs, and at one time the so-called nuts were used as food by early American tribes. At home in moist thickets in eastern and mideastern parts of the United States, the hog-peanut plant is a wild, beanlike vine. Its leaves are divided into three leaflets, and it bears two kinds of flowers. There are racemes of purplish flowers, which sprout from the twining stem; they produce small pods that seldom ripen. There also are strange flowers that grow from creeping branches at the base of the plant; they may be on, or just below, the earth's surface. They have no petals and are self-fertilizing. When a flower matures, a pear-shaped pod is formed, and it contains a single seed, the hog peanut.

PECAN

The central South of the United States is the only area in the world where the pecan grows as a wild tree. It is the largest member of the hickory family; its usual height is about seventy-five feet, though some wild trees have a recorded height of one hundred and sixty feet. Today under cultivation on plantations, pecans are commercially important because of the nuts they bear. As a result of selective growing, a nut with a paper-thin shell is now marketed; the edible kernel has a very high fat content. The meat is eaten raw, straight from the shell, or it may be salted. Pecans also are used in all sorts of baked goods.

The leaves of the pecan are up to eighteen inches in overall length; each one is made up of nine to seventeen

leaflets that have saw-toothed edges. Usually blossoming in June, the pollen-bearing male flowers grow in catkins. At the tip of a young branch there are several female flowers whose ovaries, after pollination, will in time be the seeds of the tree—the nuts. A thin, oblong husk, about two inches long, encloses the nut shell containing the kernel; when the fruit is ripe, the husk splits into four sections to release the nut.

The pecan is the state tree of Texas.

PINE NUT

Piñon

There are several species of evergreens that have edible seeds. Given the name of pine nuts, these seeds are rich in oil, starch, and sugar. Native American tribes, who gather them for food, eat the nuts raw or after parching them on hot stones.

The Rocky Mountain pine nut is a species that flourishes on mountain slopes in many areas of the Southwest. When this tree is young, it is somewhat bushy; a fully grown tree, with horizontal branches and a rounded top, may reach a height of forty feet. Its rigid leaves grow in bundles of two or, infrequently, three; each is only about one and one-half inches long. These needles are long-lived and may remain on the tree for seven or more years. The female flowers grow at the ends of branches, with catkins of male flowers nearby. A fertilized female flower is the beginning of a pine cone, which will reach maturity by the second autumn; then

it will be about one and one-half inches long. Not all the seeds under the thick scales of the roundish cone will reach the nut stage; those that do are egg shaped and are about one-half inch long. Covering the meat of the nut is a thin, brittle shell.

A related nut pine, the one-leaf piñon, is the state tree of Nevada.

Sometimes the shells of the pistachio nuts sold in stores are their natural, light-brown color; more often, after having been roasted and salted, they are colored with a vegetable dye. This coating usually is bright red, though sometimes other colors are used. The meat inside the woody shell is greenish in color and is noted for its sweet and delicate flavor. It is a favorite ingredient in confectionery and in ice cream. When mature, the nut is about three quarters of an inch long; its shell splits into two valves.

The flowers of the pistachio tree grow in racemes; female flowers grow on one tree, the male flowers on another. They are strange, greenish brown blossoms that have no petals. The pollen-bearing male flowers have five stamens set in a calyx that is like a five-sided cup. The style of the female flower is split into three parts connected to a single ovary.

On plantations, a male tree is planted among the female trees; this association ensures the formation of the nuts.

The cultivated pistachio tree grows to a height of about twenty feet. Each of its leaves is made up of three to five broad leaflets. The tree had its origin in western Asia, but flourishing orchards are now grown in many regions where the summers are hot and dry. The pistachio is closely related to the cashew.

WALNUT, BLACK

The black walnut, found east of the Rocky Mountains, is now less plentiful than it once was. Many years ago whole forests of the trees were cut down to clear land and to obtain their strong, beautiful wood. The timber is valued for making furniture and for gunstocks. Long ago, trees one hundred and fifty feet in height were not uncommon; now the average height is about one hundred feet. The descriptive name of black comes from the dark color of the tree's bark and wood.

male flower

This walnut's big compound leaves are made up of fifteen to twenty-three leaflets; often the tip leaflet is missing. The male flowers are massed on strings about three inches long, and spikes of from two to five female flowers are borne nearby. Wind carries the pollen to them and fertilizes them.

female flower

As a female flower matures, its green fruit becomes a round or oblong seed-containing husk, up to two inches in diameter. Inside it, there is a grooved, two-valved, woody shell protecting the lobed and wrinkled seed. This seed is the meat of the nut, and it is rich in oil. Dye is sometimes extracted from the bitter husks. People and animals enjoy walnut meat, which ranks high as a nutritious food. The nuts were an important source of food for native American tribes.

The walnut seen in markets usually is the English walnut. Its shell is easy to crack, and it contains more meat than the black walnut. This nut is imported or grown in California; its original home was in Asia.

WALNUT, WHITE

Butternut, Oil nut

The white walnut is referred to equally often as the butternut. By either name it is well-known for the fat that makes up much of its sweet kernel. When pressed, the meat yields a useful oil. Over the kernel is a ridged, woody shell, which, in turn, is protected by a gummy, green husk. This husk does not split open at maturity. Sometimes the nut, husk and all, is pickled in spiced vinegar for table use. Extracts from the husks and the bark of the tree are used as a vegetable dye. Sugar, with an excellent flavor, can be made from the sap.

The floral pattern of the white walnut is similar to that of its relative, the black walnut. The oblong fruits, borne three to five in a cluster, are up to two and one-half inches long. The tree's compound, slightly hairy leaves have seven or more broadish leaflets; they ooze a clammy sap. With wide-spreading branches, the butternut may reach a height of eighty feet. It grows in many parts of North America east of the Rocky Mountains.

WATER CHINQUAPIN

Water chestnut, American lotus, Yellow nelumbo

Commonly named the water chinquapin, this relative of the water lily has several local names. It grows in ponds and slow streams in the eastern and mideastern parts of the United States. Its edible seeds often are referred to as nuts; they are somewhat similar to acorns in appearance. The pod that holds them is shaped like a flat-topped cone; it has a perforated cover over holes in the pod. A seed grows below each opening and, as it grows, becomes larger than the outlet above it. Thus, the seeds cannot be released until the pod has disintegrated in the water into which it has fallen. Acting as a boat, the pod often carries its cargo far from the parent plant before the seeds are freed.

The pale yellow flowers, which produce the seed-holding pods, are about eight inches across and have many petals.

They are borne on very long stalks and bloom high above the water. The long-stemmed, roundish leaves are a foot or more across. Each is depressed at its center, where the leaf is attached to its long stem. The tubers from which the flowers and leafstalks sprout also are edible.

WITCH HAZEL NUT, AMERICAN

The American witch hazel usually grows as a many-stemmed shrub that may reach a height of twelve feet; occasionally it may be in the form of a thirty-foot tree. The leaves, two to five inches long, have coarsely toothed edges. The shrub has a number of strange characteristics. Some people think that the word *witch* in the name comes from the old belief that a hand-held, forked twig would locate water beneath the earth's surface by turning downward at that spot. The person holding the twig was known as a *water witch*. Early settlers valued the shrub because American tribesmen told them that the juice from fresh leaves and twigs was good for bruises. Today extract of witch hazel is sold in pharmacies as a lotion.

At the beginning of winter, witch hazel puts on a surprising show. The shrub's yellow flowers sprout astonishingly from the bare twigs or from twigs to which withered leaves cling. Each tiny flower has four ribbonlike, crumpled petals, no more than three quarters of an inch in length. The calyx

flower

immature capsules

is four-parted, and there are four pollen-bearing stamens. The ovary, with two cells, matures very slowly. Finally it ripens and forms a woody capsule about one-half-inch long, inside of which are two shiny, nutlike seeds.

The developing capsule remains on the twig until new flowers appear the following year. Then, one frosty day, the brown pods explode and, with a popping sound, discharge the nuts. The horny lining of the capsule contracts to shoot out the seeds; they are ejected with such force that they may come to earth as much as twenty-five feet away from the parent tree.

The American witch hazel grows wild in eastern North America.

LIST OF NUTS

Acorn   9
Almond   12
Beech nut   13
Betel nut   14
Bladdernut, American   15
Brazil nut   16
Buckeye
  (Ohio and sweet)   18
Candlenut   20
Cashew nut   22
Chestnut, American   24
Chinquapin, common   26
Coconut   27
Coconut, Seychelles   30
Cola nut   32
Ginkgo nut   33
Hazelnut   35

Hickory nut   37
Horse chestnut   39
Ivory nut   41
Litchi nut   42
Macadamia nut   43
Monkey-puzzle nut   45
Nut grass, chufa   47
Nutmeg   48
Peanut   49
Peanut, hog   50
Pecan   51
Pine nut   53
Pistachio nut   55
Walnut, black   57
Walnut, white   59
Water chinquapin   60
Witch hazel nut, American   62